BIRD WATCHING
Logbook

This Book Belongs To:

_____

_____

_____

Date:_____ Time: _____
Location:_____

Season:

◯ Spring ◯ Summer ◯ Winter ◯ Autumn

Weather:

◯ Sunny ◯ Dry ◯ Stormy ◯ Rainy
◯ Cloudy ◯ Snowy

Description:

☐ Male ☐ Female

Main color: _____
Secondary colors: _____
Wings:_____
Head: _____
Tail: _____
Beak: _____
Other: _____
_____

How many? _____
Accompanied by any other species?_____
_____

Notes:_____
_____
_____
_____
_____

Date:_____ Time: _____
Location:_____

Season:
- ○ Spring ○ Summer ○ Winter ○ Autumn

Weather:
- ○ Sunny ○ Dry ○ Stormy ○ Rainy
- ○ Cloudy ○ Snowy

Description:
- ☐ Male ☐ Female

Main color: _____
Secondary colors: _____
Wings:_____
Head: _____
Tail: _____
Beak: _____
Other: _____
_____

How many? _____
Accompanied by any other species?_____
_____

Notes:_____
_____
_____
_____
_____

Date:_____ Time: _____
Location:_____

Season:
○ Spring ○ Summer ○ Winter ○ Autumn

Weather:
○ Sunny ○ Dry ○ Stormy ○ Rainy
○ Cloudy ○ Snowy

Description:
☐ Male   ☐ Female

Main color: _____
Secondary colors: _____
Wings:_____
Head: _____
Tail: _____
Beak: _____
Other: _____
_____

How many? _____
Accompanied by any other species?_____
_____

Notes:_____
_____
_____
_____
_____

Date:_____ Time: _____
Location:_____

Season:
- ⚪ Spring ⚪ Summer ⚪ Winter ⚪ Autumn

Weather:
- ⚪ Sunny ⚪ Dry ⚪ Stormy ⚪ Rainy
- ⚪ Cloudy ⚪ Snowy

Description:
- ☐ Male ☐ Female

Main color: _____
Secondary colors: _____
Wings:_____
Head: _____
Tail: _____
Beak: _____
Other: _____
_____

How many? _____
Accompanied by any other species?_____
_____

Notes:_____
_____
_____
_____
_____

Date:_____ Time: _____
Location:_____

Season:
- ◯ Spring ◯ Summer ◯ Winter ◯ Autumn

Weather:
- ◯ Sunny ◯ Dry ◯ Stormy ◯ Rainy
- ◯ Cloudy ◯ Snowy

Description:
- ☐ Male ☐ Female

Main color: _____
Secondary colors: _____
Wings:_____
Head: _____
Tail: _____
Beak: _____
Other: _____
_____

How many? _____
Accompanied by any other species?_____
_____

Notes:_____
_____
_____
_____
_____

Date:_____ Time: _____
Location:_____

Season:
○ Spring ○ Summer ○ Winter ○ Autumn

Weather:
○ Sunny ○ Dry ○ Stormy ○ Rainy
○ Cloudy ○ Snowy

Description:
☐ Male ☐ Female

Main color: _____
Secondary colors: _____
Wings:_____
Head: _____
Tail: _____
Beak: _____
Other: _____
_____

How many? _____
Accompanied by any other species?_____
_____

Notes:_____
_____
_____
_____
_____

Date:_____ Time: _____
Location:_____

Season:
○ Spring ○ Summer ○ Winter ○ Autumn

Weather:
○ Sunny ○ Dry ○ Stormy ○ Rainy
○ Cloudy ○ Snowy

Description:
☐ Male ☐ Female

Main color: _____
Secondary colors: _____
Wings:_____
Head: _____
Tail: _____
Beak: _____
Other: _____
_____

How many? _____
Accompanied by any other species?_____
_____

Notes:_____
_____
_____
_____
_____

Date:_____ Time: _____
Location:_____

Season:
○ Spring   ○ Summer   ○ Winter   ○ Autumn

Weather:
○ Sunny   ○ Dry   ○ Stormy   ○ Rainy
○ Cloudy   ○ Snowy

Description:
☐ Male   ☐ Female

Main color: _____
Secondary colors: _____
Wings:_____
Head: _____
Tail: _____
Beak: _____
Other: _____
_____

How many? _____
Accompanied by any other species?_____
_____

Notes:_____
_____
_____
_____
_____

Date:_____ Time: _____
Location:_____

Season:
○ Spring ○ Summer ○ Winter ○ Autumn

Weather:
○ Sunny ○ Dry ○ Stormy ○ Rainy
○ Cloudy ○ Snowy

Description:
☐ Male ☐ Female

Main color: _____
Secondary colors: _____
Wings:_____
Head: _____
Tail: _____
Beak: _____
Other: _____
_____

How many? _____
Accompanied by any other species?_____
_____

Notes:_____
_____
_____
_____
_____

Date:_____ Time: _____
Location:_____

Season:
○ Spring ○ Summer ○ Winter ○ Autumn

Weather:
○ Sunny ○ Dry ○ Stormy ○ Rainy
○ Cloudy ○ Snowy

Description:
☐ Male   ☐ Female

Main color: _____
Secondary colors: _____
Wings:_____
Head: _____
Tail: _____
Beak: _____
Other: _____
_____

How many? _____
Accompanied by any other species?_____
_____

Notes:_____
_____
_____
_____
_____

Date:_____ Time: _____
Location:_____

Season:
- ⃝ Spring ⃝ Summer ⃝ Winter ⃝ Autumn

Weather:
- ⃝ Sunny ⃝ Dry ⃝ Stormy ⃝ Rainy
- ⃝ Cloudy ⃝ Snowy

Description:
☐ Male   ☐ Female

Main color: _____
Secondary colors: _____
Wings:_____
Head: _____
Tail: _____
Beak: _____
Other: _____
_____

How many? _____
Accompanied by any other species?_____
_____

Notes:_____
_____
_____
_____
_____

Date:_____ Time: _____
Location:_____

Season:
- ○ Spring   ○ Summer   ○ Winter   ○ Autumn

Weather:
- ○ Sunny   ○ Dry   ○ Stormy   ○ Rainy
- ○ Cloudy   ○ Snowy

Description:
- ☐ Male   ☐ Female

Main color: _____
Secondary colors: _____
Wings:_____
Head: _____
Tail: _____
Beak: _____
Other: _____
_____

How many? _____
Accompanied by any other species?_____
_____

Notes:_____
_____
_____
_____
_____

Date:_____ Time: _____
Location:_____

Season:
- ○ Spring ○ Summer ○ Winter ○ Autumn

Weather:
- ○ Sunny ○ Dry ○ Stormy ○ Rainy
- ○ Cloudy ○ Snowy

Description:
- ☐ Male   ☐ Female

Main color: _____
Secondary colors: _____
Wings:_____
Head: _____
Tail: _____
Beak: _____
Other: _____
_____

How many? _____
Accompanied by any other species?_____
_____

Notes:_____
_____
_____
_____
_____

Date:_____ Time: _____
Location:_____

Season:
○ Spring ○ Summer ○ Winter ○ Autumn

Weather:
○ Sunny ○ Dry ○ Stormy ○ Rainy
○ Cloudy ○ Snowy

Description:
☐ Male ☐ Female

Main color: _____
Secondary colors: _____
Wings:_____
Head: _____
Tail: _____
Beak: _____
Other: _____
_____

How many? _____
Accompanied by any other species?_____
_____

Notes:_____
_____
_____
_____
_____

Date:_____ Time: _____
Location:_____

Season:
- ◯ Spring ◯ Summer ◯ Winter ◯ Autumn

Weather:
- ◯ Sunny ◯ Dry ◯ Stormy ◯ Rainy
- ◯ Cloudy ◯ Snowy

Description:
- ☐ Male ☐ Female

Main color: _____
Secondary colors: _____
Wings:_____
Head: _____
Tail: _____
Beak: _____
Other: _____
_____

How many? _____
Accompanied by any other species?_____
_____

Notes:_____
_____
_____
_____
_____

Date:_____ Time: _____
Location:_____

Season:
○ Spring ○ Summer ○ Winter ○ Autumn

Weather:
○ Sunny ○ Dry ○ Stormy ○ Rainy
○ Cloudy ○ Snowy

Description:
☐ Male ☐ Female

Main color: _____
Secondary colors: _____
Wings:_____
Head: _____
Tail: _____
Beak: _____
Other: _____
_____

How many? _____
Accompanied by any other species?_____
_____

Notes:_____
_____
_____
_____
_____

Date:_____ Time: _____
Location:_____

Season:
○ Spring ○ Summer ○ Winter ○ Autumn

Weather:
○ Sunny ○ Dry ○ Stormy ○ Rainy
○ Cloudy ○ Snowy

Description:
☐ Male ☐ Female

Main color: _____
Secondary colors: _____
Wings:_____
Head: _____
Tail: _____
Beak: _____
Other: _____
_____

How many? _____
Accompanied by any other species?_____
_____

Notes:_____
_____
_____
_____
_____

Date:_____ Time: _____
Location:_____

Season:
- ○ Spring ○ Summer ○ Winter ○ Autumn

Weather:
- ○ Sunny ○ Dry ○ Stormy ○ Rainy
- ○ Cloudy ○ Snowy

Description:
- ☐ Male   ☐ Female

Main color: _____
Secondary colors: _____
Wings:_____
Head: _____
Tail: _____
Beak: _____
Other: _____
_____

How many? _____
Accompanied by any other species?_____
_____

Notes:_____
_____
_____
_____
_____

Date:_____ Time: _____
Location:_____

Season:
○ Spring ○ Summer ○ Winter ○ Autumn

Weather:
○ Sunny ○ Dry ○ Stormy ○ Rainy
○ Cloudy ○ Snowy

Description:
☐ Male ☐ Female

Main color: _____
Secondary colors: _____
Wings:_____
Head: _____
Tail: _____
Beak: _____
Other: _____
_____

How many? _____
Accompanied by any other species?_____
_____

Notes:_____
_____
_____
_____
_____

Date:_____ Time: _____
Location:_____

Season:
- ○ Spring ○ Summer ○ Winter ○ Autumn

Weather:
- ○ Sunny ○ Dry ○ Stormy ○ Rainy
- ○ Cloudy ○ Snowy

Description:
- ☐ Male ☐ Female

Main color: _____
Secondary colors: _____
Wings:_____
Head: _____
Tail: _____
Beak: _____
Other: _____
_____

How many? _____
Accompanied by any other species?_____
_____

Notes:_____
_____
_____
_____
_____

Date:_____ Time: _____
Location:_____

Season:
○ Spring ○ Summer ○ Winter ○ Autumn

Weather:
○ Sunny ○ Dry ○ Stormy ○ Rainy
○ Cloudy ○ Snowy

Description:
☐ Male ☐ Female

Main color: _____
Secondary colors: _____
Wings:_____
Head: _____
Tail: _____
Beak: _____
Other: _____
_____

How many? _____
Accompanied by any other species?_____
_____

Notes:_____
_____
_____
_____
_____

Date:_____ Time: _____
Location:_____

Season:
◯ Spring ◯ Summer ◯ Winter ◯ Autumn

Weather:
◯ Sunny ◯ Dry ◯ Stormy ◯ Rainy
◯ Cloudy ◯ Snowy

Description:
☐ Male ☐ Female

Main color: _____
Secondary colors: _____
Wings:_____
Head: _____
Tail: _____
Beak: _____
Other: _____
_____

How many? _____
Accompanied by any other species?_____
_____

Notes:_____
_____
_____
_____
_____

Date:_____ Time: _____
Location:_____

Season:
◯ Spring   ◯ Summer   ◯ Winter   ◯ Autumn

Weather:
◯ Sunny   ◯ Dry   ◯ Stormy   ◯ Rainy
◯ Cloudy   ◯ Snowy

Description:
☐ Male   ☐ Female

Main color: _____
Secondary colors: _____
Wings:_____
Head: _____
Tail: _____
Beak: _____
Other: _____
_____

How many? _____
Accompanied by any other species?_____
_____

Notes:_____
_____
_____
_____
_____

Date:_____ Time: _____
Location:_____

Season:
○ Spring ○ Summer ○ Winter ○ Autumn

Weather:
○ Sunny ○ Dry ○ Stormy ○ Rainy
○ Cloudy ○ Snowy

Description:
☐ Male ☐ Female

Main color: _____
Secondary colors: _____
Wings:_____
Head: _____
Tail: _____
Beak: _____
Other: _____
_____

How many? _____
Accompanied by any other species?_____
_____

Notes:_____
_____
_____
_____
_____

Date:_____ Time: _____
Location:_____

Season:
○ Spring ○ Summer ○ Winter ○ Autumn

Weather:
○ Sunny ○ Dry ○ Stormy ○ Rainy
○ Cloudy ○ Snowy

Description:
☐ Male ☐ Female

Main color: _____
Secondary colors: _____
Wings:_____
Head: _____
Tail: _____
Beak: _____
Other: _____
_____

How many? _____
Accompanied by any other species?_____
_____

Notes:_____
_____
_____
_____
_____

Date:_____ Time: _____
Location:_____

Season:
- ⊙ Spring ⊙ Summer ⊙ Winter ⊙ Autumn

Weather:
- ⊙ Sunny ⊙ Dry ⊙ Stormy ⊙ Rainy
- ⊙ Cloudy ⊙ Snowy

Description:
- ☐ Male ☐ Female

Main color: _____
Secondary colors: _____
Wings:_____
Head: _____
Tail: _____
Beak: _____
Other: _____
_____

How many? _____
Accompanied by any other species?_____
_____

Notes:_____
_____
_____
_____
_____

Date:_____ Time: _____
Location:_____

Season:
- ⭕ Spring ⭕ Summer ⭕ Winter ⭕ Autumn

Weather:
- ⭕ Sunny ⭕ Dry ⭕ Stormy ⭕ Rainy
- ⭕ Cloudy ⭕ Snowy

Description:
- ☐ Male ☐ Female

Main color: _____
Secondary colors: _____
Wings:_____
Head: _____
Tail: _____
Beak: _____
Other: _____
_____

How many? _____
Accompanied by any other species?_____
_____

Notes:_____
_____
_____
_____
_____

Date:_____ Time: _____
Location:_____

Season:
- ○ Spring ○ Summer ○ Winter ○ Autumn

Weather:
- ○ Sunny ○ Dry ○ Stormy ○ Rainy
- ○ Cloudy ○ Snowy

Description:
- ☐ Male ☐ Female

Main color: _____
Secondary colors: _____
Wings:_____
Head: _____
Tail: _____
Beak: _____
Other: _____
_____

How many? _____
Accompanied by any other species?_____
_____

Notes:_____
_____
_____
_____
_____

Date:_____ Time: _____
Location:_____

Season:
○ Spring   ○ Summer   ○ Winter   ○ Autumn

Weather:
○ Sunny   ○ Dry   ○ Stormy   ○ Rainy
○ Cloudy   ○ Snowy

Description:
☐ Male   ☐ Female

Main color: _____
Secondary colors: _____
Wings:_____
Head: _____
Tail: _____
Beak: _____
Other: _____
_____

How many? _____
Accompanied by any other species?_____
_____

Notes:_____
_____
_____
_____
_____

Date:_____ Time: _____
Location:_____

Season:
- ○ Spring ○ Summer ○ Winter ○ Autumn

Weather:
- ○ Sunny ○ Dry ○ Stormy ○ Rainy
- ○ Cloudy ○ Snowy

Description:
☐ Male   ☐ Female

Main color: _____
Secondary colors: _____
Wings:_____
Head: _____
Tail: _____
Beak: _____
Other: _____
_____

How many? _____
Accompanied by any other species?_____
_____

Notes:_____
_____
_____
_____
_____

Date:_____ Time: _____
Location:_____

Season:
○ Spring ○ Summer ○ Winter ○ Autumn

Weather:
○ Sunny ○ Dry ○ Stormy ○ Rainy
○ Cloudy ○ Snowy

Description:
☐ Male ☐ Female

Main color: _____
Secondary colors: _____
Wings:_____
Head: _____
Tail: _____
Beak: _____
Other: _____
_____

How many? _____
Accompanied by any other species?_____
_____

Notes:_____
_____
_____
_____
_____

Date:_____ Time: _____
Location:_____

Season:
- ◯ Spring ◯ Summer ◯ Winter ◯ Autumn

Weather:
- ◯ Sunny ◯ Dry ◯ Stormy ◯ Rainy
- ◯ Cloudy ◯ Snowy

Description:
☐ Male   ☐ Female

Main color: _____
Secondary colors: _____
Wings:_____
Head: _____
Tail: _____
Beak: _____
Other: _____
_____

How many? _____
Accompanied by any other species?_____
_____

Notes:_____
_____
_____
_____
_____

Date:_____ Time: _____
Location:_____

Season:
○ Spring ○ Summer ○ Winter ○ Autumn

Weather:
○ Sunny   ○ Dry   ○ Stormy   ○ Rainy
○ Cloudy   ○ Snowy

Description:
☐ Male   ☐ Female

Main color: _____
Secondary colors: _____
Wings:_____
Head: _____
Tail: _____
Beak: _____
Other: _____
_____

How many? _____
Accompanied by any other species?_____
_____

Notes:_____
_____
_____
_____
_____

Date:_____ Time: _____
Location:_____

Season:
- ○ Spring ○ Summer ○ Winter ○ Autumn

Weather:
- ○ Sunny ○ Dry ○ Stormy ○ Rainy
- ○ Cloudy ○ Snowy

Description:
- ☐ Male ☐ Female

Main color: _____
Secondary colors: _____
Wings:_____
Head: _____
Tail: _____
Beak: _____
Other: _____
_____

How many? _____
Accompanied by any other species?_____
_____

Notes:_____
_____
_____
_____
_____

Date:_____ Time: _____
Location:_____

Season:
○ Spring ○ Summer ○ Winter ○ Autumn

Weather:
○ Sunny ○ Dry ○ Stormy ○ Rainy
○ Cloudy ○ Snowy

Description:
☐ Male ☐ Female

Main color: _____
Secondary colors: _____
Wings:_____
Head: _____
Tail: _____
Beak: _____
Other: _____
_____

How many? _____
Accompanied by any other species?_____
_____

Notes:_____
_____
_____
_____
_____

Date:_____ Time: _____
Location:_____

Season:
- ○ Spring ○ Summer ○ Winter ○ Autumn

Weather:
- ○ Sunny ○ Dry ○ Stormy ○ Rainy
- ○ Cloudy ○ Snowy

Description:
- ☐ Male ☐ Female

Main color: _____
Secondary colors: _____
Wings:_____
Head: _____
Tail: _____
Beak: _____
Other: _____
_____

How many? _____
Accompanied by any other species?_____
_____

Notes:_____
_____
_____
_____
_____

Date:_____ Time: _____
Location:_____

Season:
○ Spring   ○ Summer   ○ Winter   ○ Autumn

Weather:
○ Sunny   ○ Dry   ○ Stormy   ○ Rainy
○ Cloudy   ○ Snowy

Description:
☐ Male   ☐ Female

Main color: _____
Secondary colors: _____
Wings:_____
Head: _____
Tail: _____
Beak: _____
Other: _____
_____

How many? _____
Accompanied by any other species?_____
_____

Notes:_____
_____
_____
_____
_____

Date:_____ Time: _____
Location:_____

Season:
- ○ Spring   ○ Summer   ○ Winter   ○ Autumn

Weather:
- ○ Sunny   ○ Dry   ○ Stormy   ○ Rainy
- ○ Cloudy   ○ Snowy

Description:
- ☐ Male   ☐ Female

Main color: _____
Secondary colors: _____
Wings:_____
Head: _____
Tail: _____
Beak: _____
Other: _____
_____

How many? _____
Accompanied by any other species?_____
_____

Notes:_____
_____
_____
_____
_____

Date:_____ Time: _____
Location:_____

Season:
○ Spring ○ Summer ○ Winter ○ Autumn

Weather:
○ Sunny ○ Dry ○ Stormy ○ Rainy
○ Cloudy ○ Snowy

Description:
☐ Male ☐ Female

Main color: _____
Secondary colors: _____
Wings:_____
Head: _____
Tail: _____
Beak: _____
Other: _____
_____

How many? _____
Accompanied by any other species?_____
_____

Notes:_____
_____
_____
_____
_____

Date:_____ Time: _____
Location:_____

Season:
- ◯ Spring ◯ Summer ◯ Winter ◯ Autumn

Weather:
- ◯ Sunny ◯ Dry ◯ Stormy ◯ Rainy
- ◯ Cloudy ◯ Snowy

Description:
☐ Male ☐ Female

Main color: _____
Secondary colors: _____
Wings:_____
Head: _____
Tail: _____
Beak: _____
Other: _____
_____

How many? _____
Accompanied by any other species?_____
_____

Notes:_____
_____
_____
_____
_____

Date:_____ Time: _____
Location:_____

Season:
○ Spring ○ Summer ○ Winter ○ Autumn

Weather:
○ Sunny ○ Dry ○ Stormy ○ Rainy
○ Cloudy ○ Snowy

Description:
☐ Male ☐ Female

Main color: _____
Secondary colors: _____
Wings:_____
Head: _____
Tail: _____
Beak: _____
Other: _____
_____

How many? _____
Accompanied by any other species?_____
_____

Notes:_____
_____
_____
_____
_____

Date: _____ Time: _____
Location: _____

Season:
○ Spring ○ Summer ○ Winter ○ Autumn

Weather:
○ Sunny ○ Dry ○ Stormy ○ Rainy
○ Cloudy ○ Snowy

Description:
☐ Male ☐ Female

Main color: _____
Secondary colors: _____
Wings: _____
Head: _____
Tail: _____
Beak: _____
Other: _____
_____

How many? _____
Accompanied by any other species? _____
_____

Notes: _____
_____
_____
_____
_____

Date:_____ Time: _____
Location:_____

Season:
☐ Spring ☐ Summer ☐ Winter ☐ Autumn

Weather:
☐ Sunny ☐ Dry ☐ Stormy ☐ Rainy
☐ Cloudy ☐ Snowy

Description:
☐ Male ☐ Female

Main color: _____
Secondary colors: _____
Wings:_____
Head: _____
Tail: _____
Beak: _____
Other: _____
_____

How many? _____
Accompanied by any other species?_____
_____

Notes:_____
_____
_____
_____
_____

Date:_____ Time: _____
Location:_____

Season:
○ Spring ○ Summer ○ Winter ○ Autumn

Weather:
○ Sunny ○ Dry ○ Stormy ○ Rainy
○ Cloudy ○ Snowy

Description:
☐ Male ☐ Female

Main color: _____
Secondary colors: _____
Wings:_____
Head: _____
Tail: _____
Beak: _____
Other: _____
_____

How many? _____
Accompanied by any other species?_____
_____

Notes:_____
_____
_____
_____
_____

Date:_____ Time: _____
Location:_____

Season:
○ Spring   ○ Summer   ○ Winter   ○ Autumn

Weather:
○ Sunny   ○ Dry   ○ Stormy   ○ Rainy
○ Cloudy   ○ Snowy

Description:
☐ Male   ☐ Female

Main color: _____
Secondary colors: _____
Wings:_____
Head: _____
Tail: _____
Beak: _____
Other: _____
_____

How many? _____
Accompanied by any other species?_____
_____

Notes:_____
_____
_____
_____
_____

Date:_____ Time: _____
Location:_____

Season:
- ○ Spring ○ Summer ○ Winter ○ Autumn

Weather:
- ○ Sunny ○ Dry ○ Stormy ○ Rainy
- ○ Cloudy ○ Snowy

Description:
- ☐ Male ☐ Female

Main color: _____
Secondary colors: _____
Wings:_____
Head: _____
Tail: _____
Beak: _____
Other: _____
_____

How many? _____
Accompanied by any other species?_____
_____

Notes:_____
_____
_____
_____
_____

Date:_____ Time: _____
Location:_____

Season:
○ Spring ○ Summer ○ Winter ○ Autumn

Weather:
○ Sunny ○ Dry ○ Stormy ○ Rainy
○ Cloudy ○ Snowy

Description:
☐ Male ☐ Female

Main color: _____
Secondary colors: _____
Wings:_____
Head: _____
Tail: _____
Beak: _____
Other: _____
_____

How many? _____
Accompanied by any other species?_____
_____

Notes:_____
_____
_____
_____
_____

Date:_____ Time: _____
Location:_____

Season:
○ Spring ○ Summer ○ Winter ○ Autumn

Weather:
○ Sunny ○ Dry ○ Stormy ○ Rainy
○ Cloudy ○ Snowy

Description:
☐ Male ☐ Female

Main color: _____
Secondary colors: _____
Wings:_____
Head: _____
Tail: _____
Beak: _____
Other: _____
_____

How many? _____
Accompanied by any other species?_____
_____

Notes:_____
_____
_____
_____
_____

Date:_____ Time: _____
Location:_____

Season:
○ Spring ○ Summer ○ Winter ○ Autumn

Weather:
○ Sunny ○ Dry ○ Stormy ○ Rainy
○ Cloudy ○ Snowy

Description:
☐ Male ☐ Female

Main color: _____
Secondary colors: _____
Wings:_____
Head: _____
Tail: _____
Beak: _____
Other: _____
_____

How many? _____
Accompanied by any other species?_____
_____

Notes:_____
_____
_____
_____
_____

Date:_____ Time: _____
Location:_____

Season:
○ Spring ○ Summer ○ Winter ○ Autumn

Weather:
○ Sunny ○ Dry ○ Stormy ○ Rainy
○ Cloudy ○ Snowy

Description:
☐ Male ☐ Female

Main color: _____
Secondary colors: _____
Wings:_____
Head: _____
Tail: _____
Beak: _____
Other: _____
_____

How many? _____
Accompanied by any other species?_____
_____

Notes:_____
_____
_____
_____
_____

Date:_____ Time: _____
Location:_____

Season:
○ Spring ○ Summer ○ Winter ○ Autumn

Weather:
○ Sunny ○ Dry ○ Stormy ○ Rainy
○ Cloudy ○ Snowy

Description:
☐ Male ☐ Female

Main color: _____
Secondary colors: _____
Wings:_____
Head: _____
Tail: _____
Beak: _____
Other: _____
_____

How many? _____
Accompanied by any other species?_____
_____

Notes:_____
_____
_____
_____
_____

Date:_____ Time: _____
Location:_____

Season:
○ Spring   ○ Summer   ○ Winter   ○ Autumn

Weather:
○ Sunny   ○ Dry   ○ Stormy   ○ Rainy
○ Cloudy   ○ Snowy

Description:
☐ Male   ☐ Female

Main color: _____
Secondary colors: _____
Wings:_____
Head: _____
Tail: _____
Beak: _____
Other: _____
_____

How many? _____
Accompanied by any other species?_____
_____

Notes:_____
_____
_____
_____
_____

Date:_____ Time: _____
Location:_____

Season:
○ Spring ○ Summer ○ Winter ○ Autumn

Weather:
○ Sunny ○ Dry ○ Stormy ○ Rainy
○ Cloudy ○ Snowy

Description:
☐ Male ☐ Female

Main color: _____
Secondary colors: _____
Wings:_____
Head: _____
Tail: _____
Beak: _____
Other: _____
_____

How many? _____
Accompanied by any other species?_____
_____

Notes:_____
_____
_____
_____
_____

Date:_____ Time: _____
Location:_____

Season:
○ Spring ○ Summer ○ Winter ○ Autumn

Weather:
○ Sunny ○ Dry ○ Stormy ○ Rainy
○ Cloudy ○ Snowy

Description:
☐ Male   ☐ Female

Main color: _____
Secondary colors: _____
Wings:_____
Head: _____
Tail: _____
Beak: _____
Other: _____
_____

How many? _____
Accompanied by any other species?_____
_____

Notes:_____
_____
_____
_____
_____

Date:_____ Time: _____
Location:_____

Season:
○ Spring   ○ Summer   ○ Winter   ○ Autumn

Weather:
○ Sunny   ○ Dry   ○ Stormy   ○ Rainy
○ Cloudy   ○ Snowy

Description:
☐ Male   ☐ Female

Main color: _____
Secondary colors: _____
Wings:_____
Head: _____
Tail: _____
Beak: _____
Other: _____
_____

How many? _____
Accompanied by any other species?_____
_____

Notes:_____
_____
_____
_____
_____

Date:_____ Time: _____
Location:_____

Season:
○ Spring ○ Summer ○ Winter ○ Autumn

Weather:
○ Sunny ○ Dry ○ Stormy ○ Rainy
○ Cloudy ○ Snowy

Description:
☐ Male ☐ Female

Main color: _____
Secondary colors: _____
Wings:_____
Head: _____
Tail: _____
Beak: _____
Other: _____
_____

How many? _____
Accompanied by any other species?_____
_____

Notes:_____
_____
_____
_____
_____

Date:_____ Time: _____
Location:_____

Season:
○ Spring ○ Summer ○ Winter ○ Autumn

Weather:
○ Sunny ○ Dry ○ Stormy ○ Rainy
○ Cloudy ○ Snowy

Description:
☐ Male ☐ Female

Main color: _____
Secondary colors: _____
Wings:_____
Head: _____
Tail: _____
Beak: _____
Other: _____
_____

How many? _____
Accompanied by any other species?_____
_____

Notes:_____
_____
_____
_____
_____

Date:_____ Time: _____
Location:_____

Season:
- ○ Spring ○ Summer ○ Winter ○ Autumn

Weather:
- ○ Sunny ○ Dry ○ Stormy ○ Rainy
- ○ Cloudy ○ Snowy

Description:
- ☐ Male ☐ Female

Main color: _____
Secondary colors: _____
Wings:_____
Head: _____
Tail: _____
Beak: _____
Other: _____
_____

How many? _____
Accompanied by any other species?_____
_____

Notes:_____
_____
_____
_____
_____

Date:_____ Time: _____
Location:_____

Season:
- ○ Spring ○ Summer ○ Winter ○ Autumn

Weather:
- ○ Sunny ○ Dry ○ Stormy ○ Rainy
- ○ Cloudy ○ Snowy

Description:
- ☐ Male ☐ Female

Main color: _____
Secondary colors: _____
Wings:_____
Head: _____
Tail: _____
Beak: _____
Other: _____
_____

How many? _____
Accompanied by any other species?_____
_____

Notes:_____
_____
_____
_____
_____

Date:_____ Time: _____
Location:_____

Season:
○ Spring ○ Summer ○ Winter ○ Autumn

Weather:
○ Sunny ○ Dry ○ Stormy ○ Rainy
○ Cloudy ○ Snowy

Description:
☐ Male   ☐ Female

Main color: _____
Secondary colors: _____
Wings:_____
Head: _____
Tail: _____
Beak: _____
Other: _____
_____

How many? _____
Accompanied by any other species?_____
_____

Notes:_____
_____
_____
_____
_____

Date:_____ Time: _____
Location:_____

Season:
○ Spring ○ Summer ○ Winter ○ Autumn

Weather:
○ Sunny ○ Dry ○ Stormy ○ Rainy
○ Cloudy ○ Snowy

Description:
☐ Male ☐ Female

Main color: _____
Secondary colors: _____
Wings:_____
Head: _____
Tail: _____
Beak: _____
Other: _____
_____

How many? _____
Accompanied by any other species?_____
_____

Notes:_____
_____
_____
_____
_____

Date:_____ Time: _____
Location:_____

Season:
◯ Spring ◯ Summer ◯ Winter ◯ Autumn

Weather:
◯ Sunny ◯ Dry ◯ Stormy ◯ Rainy
◯ Cloudy ◯ Snowy

Description:
☐ Male ☐ Female

Main color: _____
Secondary colors: _____
Wings:_____
Head: _____
Tail: _____
Beak: _____
Other: _____
_____

How many? _____
Accompanied by any other species?_____
_____

Notes:_____
_____
_____
_____
_____

Date:_____ Time: _____
Location:_____

Season:

○ Spring   ○ Summer   ○ Winter   ○ Autumn

Weather:

○ Sunny   ○ Dry   ○ Stormy   ○ Rainy
○ Cloudy   ○ Snowy

Description:

☐ Male   ☐ Female

Main color: _____
Secondary colors: _____
Wings:_____
Head: _____
Tail: _____
Beak: _____
Other: _____
_____

How many? _____
Accompanied by any other species?_____
_____

Notes:_____
_____
_____
_____
_____

Date:_____ Time: _____
Location:_____

Season:
○ Spring ○ Summer ○ Winter ○ Autumn

Weather:
○ Sunny ○ Dry ○ Stormy ○ Rainy
○ Cloudy ○ Snowy

Description:
☐ Male ☐ Female

Main color: _____
Secondary colors: _____
Wings:_____
Head: _____
Tail: _____
Beak: _____
Other: _____
_____

How many? _____
Accompanied by any other species?_____
_____

Notes:_____
_____
_____
_____
_____

Date:_____ Time: _____
Location:_____

Season:
○ Spring ○ Summer ○ Winter ○ Autumn

Weather:
○ Sunny ○ Dry ○ Stormy ○ Rainy
○ Cloudy ○ Snowy

Description:
☐ Male   ☐ Female

Main color: _____
Secondary colors: _____
Wings:_____
Head: _____
Tail: _____
Beak: _____
Other: _____
_____

How many? _____
Accompanied by any other species?_____
_____

Notes:_____
_____
_____
_____
_____

Date:_____ Time: _____
Location:_____

Season:
○ Spring   ○ Summer   ○ Winter   ○ Autumn

Weather:
○ Sunny   ○ Dry   ○ Stormy   ○ Rainy
○ Cloudy   ○ Snowy

Description:
☐ Male   ☐ Female

Main color: _____
Secondary colors: _____
Wings: _____
Head: _____
Tail: _____
Beak: _____
Other: _____
_____

How many? _____
Accompanied by any other species? _____
_____

Notes: _____
_____
_____
_____
_____

Date:_____ Time: _____
Location:_____

Season:
○ Spring ○ Summer ○ Winter ○ Autumn

Weather:
○ Sunny ○ Dry ○ Stormy ○ Rainy
○ Cloudy ○ Snowy

Description:
☐ Male ☐ Female

Main color: _____
Secondary colors: _____
Wings:_____
Head: _____
Tail: _____
Beak: _____
Other: _____
_____

How many? _____
Accompanied by any other species?_____
_____

Notes:_____
_____
_____
_____
_____

Date:_____ Time: _____
Location:_____

Season:
○ Spring ○ Summer ○ Winter ○ Autumn

Weather:
○ Sunny ○ Dry ○ Stormy ○ Rainy
○ Cloudy ○ Snowy

Description:
☐ Male ☐ Female

Main color: _____
Secondary colors: _____
Wings:_____
Head: _____
Tail: _____
Beak: _____
Other: _____
_____

How many? _____
Accompanied by any other species?_____
_____

Notes:_____
_____
_____
_____
_____

Date:_____ Time: _____
Location:_____

Season:
○ Spring ○ Summer ○ Winter ○ Autumn

Weather:
○ Sunny ○ Dry ○ Stormy ○ Rainy
○ Cloudy ○ Snowy

Description:
☐ Male ☐ Female

Main color: _____
Secondary colors: _____
Wings:_____
Head: _____
Tail: _____
Beak: _____
Other: _____
_____

How many? _____
Accompanied by any other species?_____
_____

Notes:_____
_____
_____
_____
_____

Date:_____ Time: _____
Location:_____

Season:
○ Spring ○ Summer ○ Winter ○ Autumn

Weather:
○ Sunny ○ Dry ○ Stormy ○ Rainy
○ Cloudy ○ Snowy

Description:
☐ Male ☐ Female

Main color: _____
Secondary colors: _____
Wings:_____
Head: _____
Tail: _____
Beak: _____
Other: _____
_____

How many? _____
Accompanied by any other species?_____
_____

Notes:_____
_____
_____
_____
_____

Date:_____ Time: _____
Location:_____

Season:
○ Spring ○ Summer ○ Winter ○ Autumn

Weather:
○ Sunny ○ Dry ○ Stormy ○ Rainy
○ Cloudy ○ Snowy

Description:
☐ Male ☐ Female

Main color: _____
Secondary colors: _____
Wings:_____
Head: _____
Tail: _____
Beak: _____
Other: _____
_____

How many? _____
Accompanied by any other species?_____
_____

Notes:_____
_____
_____
_____
_____

Date:_____ Time: _____
Location:_____

Season:
- ○ Spring ○ Summer ○ Winter ○ Autumn

Weather:
- ○ Sunny ○ Dry ○ Stormy ○ Rainy
- ○ Cloudy ○ Snowy

Description:
- ☐ Male ☐ Female

Main color: _____
Secondary colors: _____
Wings:_____
Head: _____
Tail: _____
Beak: _____
Other: _____
_____

How many? _____
Accompanied by any other species?_____
_____

Notes:_____
_____
_____
_____
_____

Date:_____ Time: _____
Location:_____

Season:
- ◯ Spring ◯ Summer ◯ Winter ◯ Autumn

Weather:
- ◯ Sunny ◯ Dry ◯ Stormy ◯ Rainy
- ◯ Cloudy ◯ Snowy

Description:
☐ Male ☐ Female

Main color: _____
Secondary colors: _____
Wings:_____
Head: _____
Tail: _____
Beak: _____
Other: _____
_____

How many? _____
Accompanied by any other species?_____
_____

Notes:_____
_____
_____
_____
_____

Date:_____ Time: _____
Location:_____

Season:
○ Spring ○ Summer ○ Winter ○ Autumn

Weather:
○ Sunny ○ Dry ○ Stormy ○ Rainy
○ Cloudy ○ Snowy

Description:
☐ Male   ☐ Female

Main color: _____
Secondary colors: _____
Wings:_____
Head: _____
Tail: _____
Beak: _____
Other: _____
_____

How many? _____
Accompanied by any other species?_____
_____

Notes:_____
_____
_____
_____
_____

Date:_____ Time: _____
Location:_____

Season:
○ Spring ○ Summer ○ Winter ○ Autumn

Weather:
○ Sunny ○ Dry ○ Stormy ○ Rainy
○ Cloudy ○ Snowy

Description:
☐ Male ☐ Female

Main color: _____
Secondary colors: _____
Wings:_____
Head: _____
Tail: _____
Beak: _____
Other: _____
_____

How many? _____
Accompanied by any other species?_____
_____

Notes:_____
_____
_____
_____
_____

Date:_____ Time: _____
Location:_____

Season:
○ Spring ○ Summer ○ Winter ○ Autumn

Weather:
○ Sunny ○ Dry ○ Stormy ○ Rainy
○ Cloudy ○ Snowy

Description:
☐ Male ☐ Female

Main color: _____
Secondary colors: _____
Wings:_____
Head: _____
Tail: _____
Beak: _____
Other: _____
_____

How many? _____
Accompanied by any other species?_____
_____

Notes:_____
_____
_____
_____
_____

Date:_____ Time: _____
Location:_____

Season:
○ Spring ○ Summer ○ Winter ○ Autumn

Weather:
○ Sunny ○ Dry ○ Stormy ○ Rainy
○ Cloudy ○ Snowy

Description:
☐ Male ☐ Female

Main color: _____
Secondary colors: _____
Wings:_____
Head: _____
Tail: _____
Beak: _____
Other: _____
_____

How many? _____
Accompanied by any other species?_____
_____

Notes:_____
_____
_____
_____
_____

Date:_____ Time: _____
Location:_____

Season:
○ Spring ○ Summer ○ Winter ○ Autumn

Weather:
○ Sunny ○ Dry ○ Stormy ○ Rainy
○ Cloudy ○ Snowy

Description:
☐ Male ☐ Female

Main color: _____
Secondary colors: _____
Wings:_____
Head: _____
Tail: _____
Beak: _____
Other: _____
_____

How many? _____
Accompanied by any other species?_____
_____

Notes:_____
_____
_____
_____
_____

Date:_____ Time: _____
Location:_____

Season:
○ Spring ○ Summer ○ Winter ○ Autumn

Weather:
○ Sunny ○ Dry ○ Stormy ○ Rainy
○ Cloudy ○ Snowy

Description:
☐ Male ☐ Female

Main color: _____
Secondary colors: _____
Wings:_____
Head: _____
Tail: _____
Beak: _____
Other: _____
_____

How many? _____
Accompanied by any other species?_____
_____

Notes:_____
_____
_____
_____
_____

Date:_____ Time: _____
Location:_____

Season:
- ○ Spring ○ Summer ○ Winter ○ Autumn

Weather:
- ○ Sunny ○ Dry ○ Stormy ○ Rainy
- ○ Cloudy ○ Snowy

Description:
☐ Male   ☐ Female

Main color: _____
Secondary colors: _____
Wings:_____
Head: _____
Tail: _____
Beak: _____
Other: _____
_____

How many? _____
Accompanied by any other species?_____
_____

Notes:_____
_____
_____
_____
_____

Date:_____ Time: _____
Location:_____

Season:
○ Spring ○ Summer ○ Winter ○ Autumn

Weather:
○ Sunny ○ Dry ○ Stormy ○ Rainy
○ Cloudy ○ Snowy

Description:
☐ Male ☐ Female

Main color: _____
Secondary colors: _____
Wings:_____
Head: _____
Tail: _____
Beak: _____
Other: _____
_____

How many? _____
Accompanied by any other species?_____
_____

Notes:_____
_____
_____
_____
_____

Date:_____ Time: _____
Location:_____

Season:
- ○ Spring
- ○ Summer
- ○ Winter
- ○ Autumn

Weather:
- ○ Sunny
- ○ Dry
- ○ Stormy
- ○ Rainy
- ○ Cloudy
- ○ Snowy

Description:
- ☐ Male
- ☐ Female

Main color: _____
Secondary colors: _____
Wings:_____
Head: _____
Tail: _____
Beak: _____
Other: _____
_____

How many? _____
Accompanied by any other species?_____
_____

Notes:_____
_____
_____
_____
_____

Date:_____ Time: _____
Location:_____

Season:
○ Spring ○ Summer ○ Winter ○ Autumn

Weather:
○ Sunny ○ Dry ○ Stormy ○ Rainy
○ Cloudy ○ Snowy

Description:
☐ Male   ☐ Female

Main color: _____
Secondary colors: _____
Wings:_____
Head: _____
Tail: _____
Beak: _____
Other: _____
_____

How many? _____
Accompanied by any other species?_____
_____

Notes:_____
_____
_____
_____
_____

Date:_____ Time: _____
Location:_____

Season:
- ◯ Spring ◯ Summer ◯ Winter ◯ Autumn

Weather:
- ◯ Sunny ◯ Dry ◯ Stormy ◯ Rainy
- ◯ Cloudy ◯ Snowy

Description:
☐ Male   ☐ Female

Main color: _____
Secondary colors: _____
Wings: _____
Head: _____
Tail: _____
Beak: _____
Other: _____
_____

How many? _____
Accompanied by any other species? _____
_____

Notes:_____
_____
_____
_____
_____

Date:_____ Time: _____
Location:_____

Season:
- ○ Spring ○ Summer ○ Winter ○ Autumn

Weather:
- ○ Sunny ○ Dry ○ Stormy ○ Rainy
- ○ Cloudy ○ Snowy

Description:
- ☐ Male ☐ Female

Main color: _____
Secondary colors: _____
Wings:_____
Head: _____
Tail: _____
Beak: _____
Other: _____
_____

How many? _____
Accompanied by any other species?_____
_____

Notes:_____
_____
_____
_____
_____

Date:_____ Time: _____
Location:_____

Season:
- ○ Spring ○ Summer ○ Winter ○ Autumn

Weather:
- ○ Sunny ○ Dry ○ Stormy ○ Rainy
- ○ Cloudy ○ Snowy

Description:
☐ Male ☐ Female

Main color: _____
Secondary colors: _____
Wings:_____
Head: _____
Tail: _____
Beak: _____
Other: _____
_____

How many? _____
Accompanied by any other species?_____
_____

Notes:_____
_____
_____
_____
_____

Date:_____ Time: _____
Location:_____

Season:
○ Spring ○ Summer ○ Winter ○ Autumn

Weather:
○ Sunny ○ Dry ○ Stormy ○ Rainy
○ Cloudy ○ Snowy

Description:
☐ Male ☐ Female

Main color: _____
Secondary colors: _____
Wings:_____
Head: _____
Tail: _____
Beak: _____
Other: _____
_____

How many? _____
Accompanied by any other species?_____
_____

Notes:_____
_____
_____
_____
_____

Date:_____ Time: _____
Location:_____

Season:

○ Spring ○ Summer ○ Winter ○ Autumn

Weather:

○ Sunny ○ Dry ○ Stormy ○ Rainy
○ Cloudy ○ Snowy

Description:

☐ Male ☐ Female

Main color: _____
Secondary colors: _____
Wings:_____
Head: _____
Tail: _____
Beak: _____
Other: _____
_____

How many? _____
Accompanied by any other species?_____
_____

Notes:_____
_____
_____
_____
_____

Date:_____ Time: _____
Location:_____

Season:
○ Spring ○ Summer ○ Winter ○ Autumn

Weather:
○ Sunny ○ Dry ○ Stormy ○ Rainy
○ Cloudy ○ Snowy

Description:
☐ Male ☐ Female

Main color: _____
Secondary colors: _____
Wings:_____
Head: _____
Tail: _____
Beak: _____
Other: _____
_____

How many? _____
Accompanied by any other species?_____
_____

Notes:_____
_____
_____
_____
_____

Date:_____ Time: _____
Location:_____

Season:
- ○ Spring ○ Summer ○ Winter ○ Autumn

Weather:
- ○ Sunny ○ Dry ○ Stormy ○ Rainy
- ○ Cloudy ○ Snowy

Description:
☐ Male   ☐ Female

Main color: _____
Secondary colors: _____
Wings:_____
Head: _____
Tail: _____
Beak: _____
Other: _____
_____

How many? _____
Accompanied by any other species?_____
_____

Notes:_____
_____
_____
_____
_____

Date:_____ Time: _____
Location:_____

Season:
○ Spring ○ Summer ○ Winter ○ Autumn

Weather:
○ Sunny ○ Dry ○ Stormy ○ Rainy
○ Cloudy ○ Snowy

Description:
☐ Male   ☐ Female

Main color: _____
Secondary colors: _____
Wings:_____
Head: _____
Tail: _____
Beak: _____
Other: _____
_____

How many? _____
Accompanied by any other species?_____
_____

Notes:_____
_____
_____
_____
_____

Date:_____ Time: _____
Location:_____

Season:
- ◯ Spring ◯ Summer ◯ Winter ◯ Autumn

Weather:
- ◯ Sunny ◯ Dry ◯ Stormy ◯ Rainy
- ◯ Cloudy ◯ Snowy

Description:
- ☐ Male ☐ Female

Main color: _____
Secondary colors: _____
Wings:_____
Head: _____
Tail: _____
Beak: _____
Other: _____
_____

How many? _____
Accompanied by any other species?_____
_____

Notes:_____
_____
_____
_____
_____

Date:_____ Time: _____
Location:_____

Season:
○ Spring ○ Summer ○ Winter ○ Autumn

Weather:
○ Sunny ○ Dry ○ Stormy ○ Rainy
○ Cloudy ○ Snowy

Description:
☐ Male ☐ Female

Main color: _____
Secondary colors: _____
Wings:_____
Head: _____
Tail: _____
Beak: _____
Other: _____
_____

How many? _____
Accompanied by any other species?_____
_____

Notes:_____
_____
_____
_____
_____

Date:_____ Time: _____
Location:_____

Season:
- ○ Spring ○ Summer ○ Winter ○ Autumn

Weather:
- ○ Sunny ○ Dry ○ Stormy ○ Rainy
- ○ Cloudy ○ Snowy

Description:
- ☐ Male ☐ Female

Main color: _____
Secondary colors: _____
Wings:_____
Head: _____
Tail: _____
Beak: _____
Other: _____
_____

How many? _____
Accompanied by any other species?_____
_____

Notes:_____
_____
_____
_____
_____

Date:_____ Time: _____
Location:_____

Season:
- ○ Spring ○ Summer ○ Winter ○ Autumn

Weather:
- ○ Sunny ○ Dry ○ Stormy ○ Rainy
- ○ Cloudy ○ Snowy

Description:
☐ Male ☐ Female

Main color: _____
Secondary colors: _____
Wings: _____
Head: _____
Tail: _____
Beak: _____
Other: _____
_____

How many? _____
Accompanied by any other species? _____
_____

Notes: _____
_____
_____
_____
_____

Date:_____ Time: _____
Location:_____

Season:
○ Spring ○ Summer ○ Winter ○ Autumn

Weather:
○ Sunny ○ Dry ○ Stormy ○ Rainy
○ Cloudy ○ Snowy

Description:
☐ Male ☐ Female

Main color: _____
Secondary colors: _____
Wings:_____
Head: _____
Tail: _____
Beak: _____
Other: _____
_____

How many? _____
Accompanied by any other species?_____
_____

Notes:_____
_____
_____
_____
_____

Date:_____ Time: _____
Location:_____

Season:
○ Spring ○ Summer ○ Winter ○ Autumn

Weather:
○ Sunny ○ Dry ○ Stormy ○ Rainy
○ Cloudy ○ Snowy

Description:
☐ Male ☐ Female

Main color: _____
Secondary colors: _____
Wings:_____
Head: _____
Tail: _____
Beak: _____
Other: _____
_____

How many? _____
Accompanied by any other species?_____
_____

Notes:_____
_____
_____
_____
_____

Date:_____ Time: _____
Location:_____

Season:
○ Spring ○ Summer ○ Winter ○ Autumn

Weather:
○ Sunny ○ Dry ○ Stormy ○ Rainy
○ Cloudy ○ Snowy

Description:
☐ Male ☐ Female

Main color: _____
Secondary colors: _____
Wings:_____
Head: _____
Tail: _____
Beak: _____
Other: _____
_____

How many? _____
Accompanied by any other species?_____
_____

Notes:_____
_____
_____
_____
_____

Date:_____ Time: _____
Location:_____

Season:
- ○ Spring ○ Summer ○ Winter ○ Autumn

Weather:
- ○ Sunny ○ Dry ○ Stormy ○ Rainy
- ○ Cloudy ○ Snowy

Description:
- ☐ Male ☐ Female

Main color: _____
Secondary colors: _____
Wings:_____
Head: _____
Tail: _____
Beak: _____
Other: _____
_____

How many? _____
Accompanied by any other species?_____
_____

Notes:_____
_____
_____
_____
_____

Date:_____ Time: _____
Location:_____

Season:
○ Spring ○ Summer ○ Winter ○ Autumn

Weather:
○ Sunny ○ Dry ○ Stormy ○ Rainy
○ Cloudy ○ Snowy

Description:
☐ Male ☐ Female

Main color: _____
Secondary colors: _____
Wings:_____
Head: _____
Tail: _____
Beak: _____
Other: _____
_____

How many? _____
Accompanied by any other species?_____
_____

Notes:_____
_____
_____
_____
_____

Date:_____ Time: _____
Location:_____

Season:
○ Spring ○ Summer ○ Winter ○ Autumn

Weather:
○ Sunny ○ Dry ○ Stormy ○ Rainy
○ Cloudy ○ Snowy

Description:
☐ Male ☐ Female

Main color: _____
Secondary colors: _____
Wings:_____
Head: _____
Tail: _____
Beak: _____
Other: _____
_____

How many? _____
Accompanied by any other species?_____
_____

Notes:_____
_____
_____
_____
_____

Date:_____ Time: _____
Location:_____

Season:
- ○ Spring ○ Summer ○ Winter ○ Autumn

Weather:
- ○ Sunny ○ Dry ○ Stormy ○ Rainy
- ○ Cloudy ○ Snowy

Description:
☐ Male ☐ Female

Main color: _____
Secondary colors: _____
Wings:_____
Head: _____
Tail: _____
Beak: _____
Other: _____
_____

How many? _____
Accompanied by any other species?_____
_____

Notes:_____
_____
_____
_____
_____

Date:_____ Time: _____
Location:_____

Season:

○ Spring   ○ Summer   ○ Winter   ○ Autumn

Weather:

○ Sunny   ○ Dry   ○ Stormy   ○ Rainy
○ Cloudy   ○ Snowy

Description:

☐ Male   ☐ Female

Main color: _____
Secondary colors: _____
Wings:_____
Head: _____
Tail: _____
Beak: _____
Other: _____
_____

How many? _____
Accompanied by any other species?_____
_____

Notes:_____
_____
_____
_____
_____

Date:_____ Time: _____
Location:_____

Season:
○ Spring ○ Summer ○ Winter ○ Autumn

Weather:
○ Sunny ○ Dry ○ Stormy ○ Rainy
○ Cloudy ○ Snowy

Description:
☐ Male ☐ Female

Main color: _____
Secondary colors: _____
Wings:_____
Head: _____
Tail: _____
Beak: _____
Other: _____
_____

How many? _____
Accompanied by any other species?_____
_____

Notes:_____
_____
_____
_____
_____

Date:_____ Time: _____
Location:_____

Season:
- ⚪ Spring ⚪ Summer ⚪ Winter ⚪ Autumn

Weather:
- ⚪ Sunny ⚪ Dry ⚪ Stormy ⚪ Rainy
- ⚪ Cloudy ⚪ Snowy

Description:
☐ Male ☐ Female

Main color: _____
Secondary colors: _____
Wings:_____
Head: _____
Tail: _____
Beak: _____
Other: _____
_____

How many? _____
Accompanied by any other species?_____
_____

Notes:_____
_____
_____
_____
_____

Date:_____ Time: _____
Location:_____

Season:
○ Spring ○ Summer ○ Winter ○ Autumn

Weather:
○ Sunny ○ Dry ○ Stormy ○ Rainy
○ Cloudy ○ Snowy

Description:
☐ Male ☐ Female

Main color: _____
Secondary colors: _____
Wings:_____
Head: _____
Tail: _____
Beak: _____
Other: _____
_____

How many? _____
Accompanied by any other species?_____
_____

Notes:_____
_____
_____
_____
_____

Date:_____ Time: _____
Location:_____

Season:

○ Spring ○ Summer ○ Winter ○ Autumn

Weather:

○ Sunny ○ Dry ○ Stormy ○ Rainy
○ Cloudy ○ Snowy

Description:

☐ Male ☐ Female

Main color: _____
Secondary colors: _____
Wings:_____
Head: _____
Tail: _____
Beak: _____
Other: _____
_____

How many? _____
Accompanied by any other species?_____
_____

Notes:_____
_____
_____
_____
_____

Date:_____ Time: _____
Location:_____

Season:
○ Spring ○ Summer ○ Winter ○ Autumn

Weather:
○ Sunny ○ Dry ○ Stormy ○ Rainy
○ Cloudy ○ Snowy

Description:
☐ Male ☐ Female

Main color: _____
Secondary colors: _____
Wings:_____
Head: _____
Tail: _____
Beak: _____
Other: _____
_____

How many? _____
Accompanied by any other species?_____
_____

Notes:_____
_____
_____
_____
_____

Date:_____ Time: _____
Location:_____

Season:
- ○ Spring ○ Summer ○ Winter ○ Autumn

Weather:
- ○ Sunny ○ Dry ○ Stormy ○ Rainy
- ○ Cloudy ○ Snowy

Description:
- ☐ Male   ☐ Female

Main color: _____
Secondary colors: _____
Wings:_____
Head: _____
Tail: _____
Beak: _____
Other: _____
_____

How many? _____
Accompanied by any other species?_____
_____

Notes:_____
_____
_____
_____
_____

Date:_____ Time: _____
Location:_____

Season:
○ Spring ○ Summer ○ Winter ○ Autumn

Weather:
○ Sunny ○ Dry ○ Stormy ○ Rainy
○ Cloudy ○ Snowy

Description:
☐ Male ☐ Female

Main color: _____
Secondary colors: _____
Wings:_____
Head: _____
Tail: _____
Beak: _____
Other: _____
_____

How many? _____
Accompanied by any other species?_____
_____

Notes:_____
_____
_____
_____
_____

Date:_____ Time: _____
Location:_____

Season:
○ Spring ○ Summer ○ Winter ○ Autumn

Weather:
○ Sunny ○ Dry ○ Stormy ○ Rainy
○ Cloudy ○ Snowy

Description:
☐ Male ☐ Female

Main color: _____
Secondary colors: _____
Wings:_____
Head: _____
Tail: _____
Beak: _____
Other: _____
_____

How many? _____
Accompanied by any other species?_____
_____

Notes:_____
_____
_____
_____
_____

Date:_____ **Time:** _____
Location:_____

Season:
○ Spring   ○ Summer   ○ Winter   ○ Autumn

Weather:
○ Sunny   ○ Dry   ○ Stormy   ○ Rainy
○ Cloudy   ○ Snowy

Description:
☐ Male   ☐ Female

Main color: _____
Secondary colors: _____
Wings:_____
Head: _____
Tail: _____
Beak: _____
Other: _____
_____

How many? _____
Accompanied by any other species?_____
_____

Notes:_____
_____
_____
_____
_____

Date:_____ Time: _____
Location:_____

Season:
○ Spring   ○ Summer   ○ Winter   ○ Autumn

Weather:
○ Sunny   ○ Dry   ○ Stormy   ○ Rainy
○ Cloudy   ○ Snowy

Description:
☐ Male   ☐ Female

Main color: _____
Secondary colors: _____
Wings:_____
Head: _____
Tail: _____
Beak: _____
Other: _____
_____

How many? _____
Accompanied by any other species?_____
_____

Notes:_____
_____
_____
_____
_____

Date:_____ Time: _____
Location:_____

Season:
◯ Spring   ◯ Summer   ◯ Winter   ◯ Autumn

Weather:
◯ Sunny   ◯ Dry   ◯ Stormy   ◯ Rainy
◯ Cloudy   ◯ Snowy

Description:
☐ Male   ☐ Female

Main color: _____
Secondary colors: _____
Wings:_____
Head: _____
Tail: _____
Beak: _____
Other: _____
_____

How many? _____
Accompanied by any other species?_____
_____

Notes:_____
_____
_____
_____
_____

Date:_____ Time: _____
Location:_____

Season:
○ Spring ○ Summer ○ Winter ○ Autumn

Weather:
○ Sunny ○ Dry ○ Stormy ○ Rainy
○ Cloudy ○ Snowy

Description:
☐ Male ☐ Female

Main color: _____
Secondary colors: _____
Wings:_____
Head: _____
Tail: _____
Beak: _____
Other: _____
_____

How many? _____
Accompanied by any other species?_____
_____

Notes:_____
_____
_____
_____
_____

Date:_____ Time: _____
Location:_____

Season:
○ Spring ○ Summer ○ Winter ○ Autumn

Weather:
○ Sunny ○ Dry ○ Stormy ○ Rainy
○ Cloudy ○ Snowy

Description:
☐ Male ☐ Female

Main color: _____
Secondary colors: _____
Wings:_____
Head: _____
Tail: _____
Beak: _____
Other: _____
_____

How many? _____
Accompanied by any other species?_____
_____

Notes:_____
_____
_____
_____
_____

Date:_____ Time: _____
Location:_____

Season:
○ Spring ○ Summer ○ Winter ○ Autumn

Weather:
○ Sunny ○ Dry ○ Stormy ○ Rainy
○ Cloudy ○ Snowy

Description:
☐ Male ☐ Female

Main color: _____
Secondary colors: _____
Wings:_____
Head: _____
Tail: _____
Beak: _____
Other: _____
_____

How many? _____
Accompanied by any other species?_____
_____

Notes:_____
_____
_____
_____
_____

Date:_____ Time: _____
Location:_____

Season:
○ Spring ○ Summer ○ Winter ○ Autumn

Weather:
○ Sunny ○ Dry ○ Stormy ○ Rainy
○ Cloudy ○ Snowy

Description:
☐ Male ☐ Female

Main color: _____
Secondary colors: _____
Wings: _____
Head: _____
Tail: _____
Beak: _____
Other: _____
_____

How many? _____
Accompanied by any other species?_____
_____

Notes:_____
_____
_____
_____
_____

What do you think of our Book

We would be very gratteful if you could leave us a feedback.

Made in the USA
Middletown, DE
17 February 2021